The Dragon Lover

AND OTHER CHINESE PROVERBS

葉公好龍

中國成語故事五則

STORY AND PICTURES BY YONG-SHENG XUAN

文•圖 宣永生

SHEN'S
BOOKS

AUBURN • CALIFORNIA

TO MY FRIEND WILFRED DUBE.
- Y . S . X . -

SHEN'S BOOKS
8625 Hubbard Road
Auburn, California 95602-7815
800-456-6660
http://www.shens.com

Printed in Hong Kong

10 9 8 7 6 5 4 3 2 1

Library of Congress Cataloging-in-Publication Data

Xuan, Yong-sheng
The dragon lover and other Chinese proverbs/
story and pictures by Yong-sheng Xuan.
p. cm.
ISBN 1-885008-11-2
Content: The Lazy Farmer • The Crane and the Clam •
The Musician and the Water Buffalo • An Old Horse • The Dragon Lover.
1. Proverbs, Chinese. 2. Chinese language • Idioms. I. Title.
PN6519.C5X83   1999
398.2'0951'02 • dc21   98-38762   CIP

THE LAZY FARMER

守株待兔

從前有一個不愛種田的懶農夫。有一天他心不在焉的除著草，忽然看見一隻野兔從眼前竄過。他丟下了鋤頭，就追了上去。

Long ago there was a lazy farmer who would rather do anything than weed and tend to his rice fields. One day, while mindlessly tilling the ground, he saw a rabbit scurrying across the land. Throwing down his hoe, the farmer began to chase the frightened animal.

野兔左彎右拐想避開農夫的追趕。笨拙的農夫喘著氣：「看樣子追不上這隻飛兔了！」沒想到一根大樹樁正好在面前，兔子一頭撞上！轟隆一聲響，兔毛滿天飛，可憐的兔子當場倒斃！

The rabbit quickly zigzagged across the field to avoid the slow and clumsy farmer. "There's no way I'll catch that quick rabbit," the farmer gasped. But suddenly, failing to see a large tree stump in its way, the rabbit met the tree trunk head-on. With a dull thud and a cloud of fur, the rabbit broke its neck!

手拎著死兔，懶農夫想：「不費吹灰之力，正好做我的晚餐。」田裏的苦工在他眼中就更加乏味。他下定決心，每天捉一隻兔子，就再也不必流汗種田了。

Quickly grabbing the rabbit, the lazy farmer thought to himself, "This will be perfect for my dinner tonight. And best of all, I hardly had to work to get this treat." Mocking his daily chore of working in the fields, the lazy farmer then said firmly, "If I can get one rabbit each day, I will never have to sweat over these crops again."

農夫一概不理，只等著另一隻兔子來送死。

們譏笑他說：「你這個人又蠢又懶，你和你的稻子一樣的會枯死！」懶

於是，懶農夫天天守在樹樁旁。眼看著田裏日漸長滿了野草，村民

And so, as time passed, the lazy farmer stopped working. He just kept waiting by the stump. After a while his crops became visibly choked with weeds. "Look at that silly man," the villagers taunted him. "Your crops are dying, and so will you, you lazy farmer!" But the farmer just ignored their warnings, and kept waiting for another rabbit.

人來人往，除了天上徘徊的禿鷹，就不見半隻兔子。原來，愚昧的懶農夫已經餓得半死。為了只享受而不工作，他不但荒廢了田產，更斷送了自己的前途。

The villagers came and went, but no rabbit ever did, not even one. The only animal that did come was a circling vulture. You see, the lazy farmer was slowly starving to death from his own foolishness. He ruined his crops and ruined his life thinking that he could reap a harvest without doing any work.

對牛彈琴

中國古時候有位著名的琴師，經常在宮廷中演奏。全國上下不但爭相邀請他演出，更公認他為最佳的琴師。他也非常樂意為敬愛他的聽眾彈奏。

There was once a great zither player in China who appeared in many concerts for royal courts. His performances were in great demand all over the country. "You are the finest zither player in all the lands," people had complimented him. The musician always enjoyed playing music for anyone who would listen, whoever the audience might be.

一天黃昏，他在花園練著一首得意的曲子時，一頭水牛從旁慢慢走來。為了引起老牛的注意，琴師彈得更賣力。誰知老牛毫無感受，只低頭啃著四周的青草。

One evening, as he was rehearsing one of his best pieces, a water buffalo came strolling along. Playing ever so intently, the musician attempted to lure the attention of the beast. Instead, the water buffalo just continued to munch on the sweet grass around him, uninterested in the zither player's music.

撥琴聲，搖頭擺尾起來。

眼看老牛沒有反應，琴師氣餒地撥著琴弦。沒想到，老牛似乎喜歡

Irritated with his unmoved audience, the musician banged the zither strings with a huff of disappointment. To his surprise, the water buffalo looked up, wagging its tail and nodding its head, as if it liked the twangy sound.

琴師這才明白，原來他胡亂撥動琴弦，聽在老牛耳中像是蚊子的叫聲，那才是佳音！從此以後，琴師發誓只對懂得欣賞音樂的聽眾演奏了。

The zither player suddenly realized that he had created a sound like that of an evening cricket. To the animal, the sounds of insects were the sounds to appreciate! From that day on, the musician promised himself to always play the right music for the right audience.

鷸蚌相爭

在一個晴朗的日子裏，有一隻海蚌在沙灘上曬著日光浴，與同伴們張開貝殼吸取溫暖的陽光和新鮮的空氣，消遙無比。

One sunny day at the beach, a clam crawled out of the water to warm its cold shell. Basking beside its seaside friends on the smooth glistening sand, the clam quickly opened its shell to take in the sun and fresh sea air. How happy the clam was to be carefree, soaking

一隻飢餓的鷸鳥打頭上飛過，正好瞧見毫無防備的海蚌。鷸鳥俯衝而下，把又長又尖的利嘴對準了鮮嫩多汁的蚌肉，海蚌仍舒展著外殼，完全沒有注意到鷸鳥飛過沙灘的陰影。

A hungry crane flying above soon spotted the contented clam. Immediately diving toward the clam, the crane aimed its long, razor-sharp beak at the tender, juicy appetizer. Unaware of the enemy, the clam rested with its shell wide open as the crane's shadow darted swiftly across the sand.

看到這個情景，海蚌的夥伴們不由驚嚇得尖叫，說時遲，那時快，海蚌用力合攏起來，正好把鷸鳥的長嘴夾住。鷸鳥和海蚌各不相讓，雙方牢牢地卡在一起。

Shrieks of horror filled the air as the crane reached for the clam's flesh. Frightened by the commotion, the clam instantly snapped shut, right on the crane's beak. The crane and the clam were now stuck

死勁地拍著翅膀想把長嘴拔出來，鷸鳥呻吟道：「今日不下雨，明日不下雨，活活渴死你，快快放開我！」可是，海蚌不為所動。

Feverishly flapping its wings, the crane tried with all its might to pull free. Recognizing that it was indeed stuck, the crane squawked with its muffled voice, "No rain today, no rain tomorrow, you will die of thirst! Now let go of my beak!" But the clam would not budge.

吃，活活餓死你，偏不放你走！」推推擠擠地兩個打了起來。

自認佔了上風，信心十足的海蚌回答説：「今天沒得吃，明天沒得

Feeling confident that it had the upper-hand, the clam echoed back,
"No food today, no food tomorrow, you will surely die of hunger! I will
never let you go!" And so the two kept straining and jostling in battle

一個漁人悄悄地從後而來，順手活捉糾纏在一起的鷸鳥和海蚌。兩者既不相讓，漁人倒成了真正的贏家，歡歡喜喜的帶著晚餐回家了。

Soon, the argument caught the attention of a fisherman. He quietly snuck up behind the quarreling twosome and grabbed the fighting pair as they remained entangled with one another. Unwilling to give in, the crane and the clam both became losers as the fisherman set off for home to cook his prized dinner.

老馬識途

春秋戰國，英勇好戰的齊桓公常打勝仗。這次他預備去攻打一個遠方的敵國，全國上下都誓言效忠他的領導。於是，他帶著英勇壯丁和精緻的裝備共上戰場。

Once there was a daring and confident warrior, the Lord of Qi (pronounced chē), who had led many winning battles. As he began another war with a far-away enemy, his countrymen vowed undying loyalty to him. With strong horses and sharpened swords, the soldiers set off for battle.

果然，打了半年仗，齊桓公忠勇的部隊再次得勝。正準備班師回朝時，大雪紛飛，掩蓋了所有的道路。

After fighting for more than two seasons in the distant land, once again, Lord Qi led his faithful troops to victory. As they finally prepared to return home, the winter trails became packed with layer upon layer of fresh, thick snow. "The trails have disappeared!" one of the lead soldiers cried.

AN OLD HORSE

沒有多久，齊桓公的大軍就在崎嶇的山嶺中迷失了方向。他立即在谷中紮營，另派遣哨兵冒著刺骨北風，四處探尋出路。

It did not take long before Lord Qi and his troops lost their way in the rugged mountain range. Stopping in a small clearing, Lord Qi ordered the tents to be set up. The icy north wind blew harder and harder as Lord Qi sent scouts out in every direction.

探路哨兵回報的全是壞消息。
「懸崖陡壁，沒有通路！」「峽谷太深！」
「齊公，我們已盡全力，實在找不到出路！」
齊桓公憤怒的說：「我不信找不到路回去！」

The scouts came back with nothing but bad news.

"The cliffs are impassable!"

"The gorges are too deep!"

"We have done our best, Lord Qi, and we now stand at a loss."

"But, there has got to be a way home," Lord Qi bellowed.

AN OLD HORSE

經過一夜的失眠和焦慮，大臣管仲終於想起了一個古老的辦法。他建議：「找匹老馬，解開它的韁繩。老馬的直覺和本能會領它回家，我們在後面緊緊跟著。」齊桓公深信管仲的智慧，於是命令道：「立即解營！」

After a cold and sleepless night, the senior advisor to Lord Qi remembered an age-old idea. "Release an old horse from its reins. Its instincts will take it back home, and we will stay close behind it," he suggested.

Trusting the wisdom of his counsel, Lord Qi quickly ordered his troops, "Pack up your tents!"

跟著訓練有素的老馬，上山下谷，不久就走出深雪，到達了熟悉的平原。多虧老馬的好記性，齊桓公再度獲取了部隊的忠心及信任。

Through the rugged mountains and thick snow they traveled, as their oldest and most well-trained horse led them. Soon, as the snow began to clear, Lord Qi could see the familiar plains of home. Thanks to the reliable memories of an old horse, confidence in Lord Qi and the safety of his troops were both restored.

葉公好龍

春秋時，楚國有位姓葉的小縣官非常喜歡龍。他空閒時特別愛畫龍，寫龍，並吟詩讚美龍。

In a small county in the Chu province there once lived a sheriff named Yi. Sheriff Yi was infatuated with dragons. In his free time the sheriff would paint dragons, write about them, and sing praises to the mighty dragons.

不論是親友或路人，葉公與人交談總離不開龍。他著迷的程度到了無時無刻不在想龍，連晚上睡覺也會夢到龍。

Sheriff Yi would engage in conversations about dragons with friends, relatives, and even strangers. His obsession with dragons seemed to occupy every minute of his waking hours. Even his nightly dreams were of nothing but dragons.

飾，掛著的、鑲著的、裝著的、繡著的，裏裏外外都佈滿了龍。城裏人都把葉公的龍癖做為話柄。爭先搶後地到他家去參觀各種龍

The town buzzed with gossip about Sheriff Yi's love and envy of dragons. Everyone wished to tour his house, just to see the many coiling and looping dragons. There, dragon images were woven, framed, hung, and embroidered, covering everything in Sheriff Yi's house.

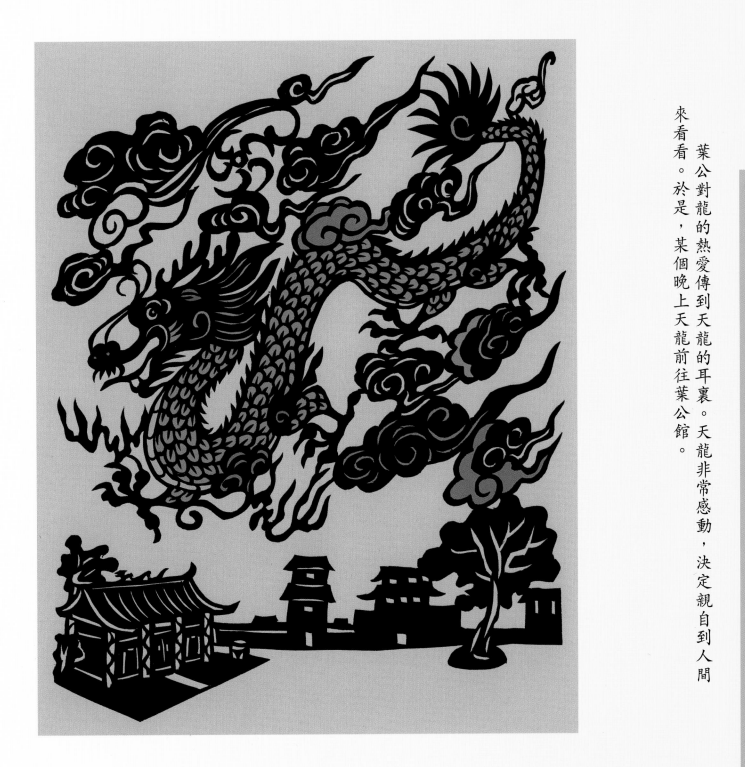

葉公對龍的熱愛傳到天龍的耳裏。天龍非常感動，決定親自到人間來看看。於是，某個晚上天龍前往葉公館。

News of Sheriff Yi's passion for dragons quickly reached the Imperial Dragon in Heaven. He was royally touched by Sheriff Yi's love for all things dragon, and decided to pay him a visit in person. One night, the Imperial Dragon set out to meet Sheriff Yi.

THE DRAGON LOVER

半夜三更，天龍下降。一走進葉家花園，天龍立即被廟宇般的裝潢吸引。龍體在大廳中迴旋了一番，天龍此刻確信葉公對龍的欽慕。

Midnight struck as the Imperial Dragon approached the earth. He landed in Sheriff Yi's garden, and was immediately in awe of the shrine-like surroundings. Twisting and twirling his long body through the living room, the Imperial Dragon could see Sheriff Yi's obvious admiration for dragons.

睡眼惺忪的葉公被屋內的聲音吵醒，更被天龍的出現嚇住了。頓時，好龍的葉公魂飛膽散，驚叫不己。沒想到，站在他眼前的是一隻活生生的龍！

Awakened by the noises, sleepy Sheriff Yi was stunned at the overwhelming sight of the Imperial Dragon. The dragon lover screamed with all his might, for here, before his eyes, was a real, living dragon.

THE DRAGON LOVER

葉公飛快的逃了出去，滿屋子的龍飾倒得倒、碎得碎。天龍不解葉公的反應，尾隨求道：「千萬別走！我不過想謝謝你對龍的虔誠罷了！」

As quickly as he could, Sheriff Yi made his way out of the house, running into and knocking down many of his beloved dragon artifacts. Confused as to why his most devoted admirer would react in such an odd way, the Imperial Dragon pleaded, "Please, please don't leave! I only wish to thank you for being my admirer."

葉公此時肝膽已破，四處嚎啕鼠竄。絕望的天龍在回程中才發覺葉公不是真的愛龍，他其實是怕龍。假裝自己愛龍往往可以掩飾真正怕龍的恐懼感。

Horror stricken, Sheriff Yi scrambled away wailing. In deep despair, the Imperial Dragon journeyed back to Heaven realizing that Sheriff Yi was not a real dragon lover. He was actually quite frightened of them, and only acted as though he admired dragons to hide his deep-rooted fear.

PUBLISHER'S NOTE

Our storytelling is based on the original texts that are found in several historical documents. Out of the vast amount of ancient text written metaphorically about animals to illustrate timeless wisdom, we feel that these five proverbs portray important truths in a meaningful way. The value of these morals is so universal that they are worth retelling to our own children, for their application to contemporary life.

《韓非子·五蠹》 宋人有耕者，田中有株，兔走觸株折頸而死。
因釋其而守株，冀復得兔，兔不可復得，而身為宋國笑。

"THE LAZY FARMER," found in *The Book of Han Fei Zi*, describes the consequences of wanting to gain something without expending any energy.

《理惑論》 公明儀為牛彈清角之操，伏食如故，非牛不聞，不合其矣。

"THE MUSICIAN AND THE WATER BUFFALO," found in *The Hongming Encyclopedia of Buddhism*, alludes to speaking to an audience in a manner which it can understand.

《戰國策·燕策二》 今者巨來，過易水，蚌方出曝，而鷸啄其肉，蚌合而拑其喙。
鷸曰：「今日不雨，明日不雨，即有死蚌。」蚌亦謂鷸曰：「今日不出，明日不出，即有死鷸。」兩者不肯相舍，漁者得而擒之。

"THE CRANE AND THE CLAM," also entitled, "The Fight Between the Snipe and the Clam," was found in *The Anecdotes of the Warring States*, tells how a third party sometimes benefits from a fight between two others, as "when two dogs fight, and a third runs away with the bone."

《韓非子·説林上》 管仲，隰朋從於桓公而伐孤竹。春往冬返，迷惑失道。
管仲曰：「老馬之智可用也。」乃放老馬而隨之，遂得道行。

"AN OLD HORSE," also found in *The Book of Han Fei Zi*, describes how someone who is very wise or experienced can be of great value in a time of need.

《新序·雜事》 葉公子高好龍，鈎以寫龍，鑿以寫龍，屋室雕文以寫龍。
於是天龍聞而下之，窺頭于牖，施尾於堂。葉公見之，棄而還走，失其魂魄，五色無主。
是葉公非好龍也，好夫似龍而非龍者也。

"THE DRAGON LOVER," found in *The Book of New Discourses*, tells of a person who has a professed love for something when in reality their honest feelings are of great fear. It is similar to that of "One who praises the sea, but keeps to the land."